Self-esteem at the Centre

The **M**odel, **O**pportunity **T**each Approach
to raise self-esteem and emotional literacy

George Robinson and Barbara Maines

P·C·P
Paul Chapman
Publishing

Lucky Duck is more than a publishing house and training agency. George Robinson and Barbara Maines founded the company in the 1980s when they worked together as a head and as a psychologist, developing innovative strategies to support challenging students.

They have an international reputation for their work on bullying, self-esteem, emotional literacy and many other subjects of interest to the world of education.

George and Barbara have set up a regular news-spot on the website at http://www.luckyduck.co.uk/newsAndEvents/viewNewsItems and information about their training programmes can be found at www.insetdays.com

More details about Lucky Duck can be found at http://www.luckyduck.co.uk/

Visit the website for all our latest publications in our specialist topics

- Emotional Literacy
- Self-esteem
- Bullying
- Positive Behaviour Management
- Circle Time
- Anger Management
- Asperger's Syndrome
- Eating Disorders

ISBN: 1 904 315 35.6

Published by Lucky Duck
Paul Chapman Publishing
A SAGE Publications Company
1 Oliver's Yard
55 City Road
London EC1Y 1SP

SAGE Publications, Inc.
2455 Teller Road
Thousand Oaks, California 91320

SAGE Publications India Pvt Ltd
B-42, Panchsheel Enclave
Post Box 4109
New Delhi 110 017

www.luckyduck.co.uk

Contents

About Lucky Duck Publishing Ltd
a publishing and training company

George Robinson and Barbara Maines met in 1984 when George was the head teacher of a special school for young people with emotional and behavioural difficulties and Barbara was the educational psychologist to the school. Together they developed a radical, self-concept approach and the resulting success of their methods led to invitations to speak at training events and conferences. As the training project grew the written handouts seeded what has become a leading UK publishing house specialising in education resources on humanistic teaching methods.

They are best known for courses on Bullying, Emotional Literacy and Self-esteem. During the growth and development of the company George worked at the University of the West of England as Director of the Modular Programme in the Faculty of Education, and later as Director of the Community Action Centre. Barbara sought opportunities to spend more time with young people in difficulty and gave up her post as a psychologist to join a behaviour support team. They both gradually reduced these commitments until, by 1999 they were working full-time for Lucky Duck as publishers and trainers. Barbara and George have an international reputation as innovative, challenging and creative trainers.

Among those who help teachers to build good relationships are the people who run Lucky Duck Publishing - their list is full of books and other materials that show deep understanding of children.

Gerald Haigh T.E.S. May 2001

Lucky Duck publishes videos, books and training materials focusing on Behaviour Management, Bullying, Circle Time and Special Needs. The approach is a skilful humanitarian blend of behaviour and counselling methods and the materials are comprehensive and user-friendly.

Special Children June 1997

A Page of Quotations

Everyone has inside himself....what shall I call it....a piece of good news. Everyone is a very great and important character. Yes, that's what we have to tell them. Every man must be persuaded, even if he's in rags, that he is immensely, immensely important. Every one must respect him and make him respect himself too. They must listen to him attentively, don't stand on top of him, don't stand in his light, but look at him with gentleness, deference, give him great, great hopes, he needs them, especially if he's young...spoil him. Yes, make him grow proud.

BURNT FLOWER BED Ugo Betti. (An Italian play)

Overnight changes in your children's behaviour are not likely. After all it took a long time for them to get where they are.

100 Ways to Enhance Self-concept in the Classroom Canfield,J. & Wells,H.

LIZA. "You see, really and truly, apart from the things anyone can pick up, (the dressing and the proper way of speaking, and so on), the difference between a lady and a flower girl is not how she behaves, BUT HOW SHE IS TREATED. I shall always be a flower girl to Professor Higgins, because he always treats me as a flower girl, and always will; but I know I can be a lady to you, because you always treat me as a lady, and always will.

Pygmalion, George Bernard Shaw

Every person needs recognition. It is expressed cogently by the lad who says, "Mother, let's play darts. I'll throw the darts and you say 'Wonderful'."

M.Dale Baughman, quoted in "Glad to be Me." ed. Elkins

...you've got to help me. You've got to hold out your hand even when that's the last thing I seem to want or need. ...Each time you are kind and gentle and encouraging, each time you try to understand because you really care, my heart begins to grow wings, very small wings, very feeble wings, - but wings."

From "Glad to be Me" edited by Don Peretz Elkins.

Even the most insensitive parent or teacher can usually recognise and take into account a crippling physical handicap. Negative self-esteem however is often overlooked because we fail to take the time and effort it requires to be sensitive to how children see themselves and their abilities.

Self-concept and School Achievement. Purkey,W.

Introduction

This booklet is a new edition of the first training handout we produced, "You Can... You KNOW You Can!" first printed in 1986. The text and activities have been planned and produced to accompany our lecture/workshops which we present for adults who work with children. Whilst each workshop is different depending on the needs of the group and the time allowed, all include crucial elements around which we base our self-concept approach to meeting the needs of children with learning or behavioural difficulties. We try to make our sessions enjoyable and informative and hope to improve the experience for the participants by relieving them of the necessity to take notes and providing a record of the message we have tried to convey.

At the end of the booklet you will find a list of references and suggested reading which we think may be of interest, together with information about the other materials that we have produced. Please do contact us if you have any comments on this handout or any other aspects of our work. We are always modifying our programme and materials in an attempt to improve and make them as helpful as possible.

What do we Mean by Self-concept?

Our interest in self-concept as a determining aspect of children's learning and behaviour led us to read widely (and argue extensively) about the various theories and the terminology. In his book "Improved Reading through Counselling," (Lawrence 1973) Denis Lawrence offers a model on which we have based our thinking.

This is our version:

A person's self-concept is his perception of his unique personal characteristics such as appearance, ability, temperament, physique, attitude and beliefs. These determine his view of his position in society and his value to and relationships with other people. The development of self-concept is a continuous process which begins with a baby's earliest interaction with caring adults and continues as the child develops. The significant person in the early years is the parent, but on entering school the child begins relationships with new "significant others."

SELF-CONCEPT is an umbrella term within which we find the various aspects of our ideas about self. Each of us carries with us two pictures: the person we are and the person we would like to be.

1. The SELF-IMAGE

A child grows up with all sorts of ideas about himself, his abilities, attributes and appearance. These are acquired and influenced by his perceptions of how he is accepted and valued by the adults who care for him. This self-image goes with him at all times and influences what he does and how he behaves. There can be lots of aspects of self-image, social, physical, intellectual, and they are all influenced by the significant other in the child's life. A negative self-image is a handicap that we as significant others must recognise and try to alleviate. The environment we create for a child must not re-inforce his feelings of failure, rejection and reminders of personal inadequacies. If we could look in on a child's self-image it would resemble an album of self-portraits, sometimes candid, sometimes posed; some are detailed and some enlarged but all are close-ups, all are revealing and all are very personal.

2. The IDEAL SELF

From his interactions with "significant others" the child forms an impression of the abilities and personal qualities which are admired and valued. From these he can compose a picture of the desirable person, an "ideal self", the person he would like to be.

SELF-ESTEEM

Self-esteem might be imagined as the distance between these two pictures. If self-image is good and ideal self feels comfortably close then self-esteem is high and goals are seen as attainable and worth striving for. If self-image is poor and that ideal self is quite out of reach then self-esteem will be low and effort to improve will be regarded as futile.

We find this model helpful in our work with children because it suggests that we can improve self-concept in two ways. Firstly we can help children to have a better self-image and secondly we can create for them a realistic and attainable ideal self; we can set them goals and help them to reach those goals.

Children who have warm, affectionate relationships with parents have higher self-esteem even when they are relatively inadequate at specific skills. High self-esteem provides a child with the confidence to attempt difficult things without an incapacitating fear of failure.

A pupil with a low self-esteem finds it difficult to try new strategies. He protects what he has and continues to behave in a manner consistent with his poor view of himself. If he feels rejected and views himself as unacceptable and valueless then he doesn't regard disapproval as a reaction to his behaviour but to himself.

Attempts to work with children to improve self-esteem must offer feedback which counteracts this interpretation under conditions which are accepting and non-judgemental.

The whole process is a BEHAVIOURAL DIALOGUE between the developing self and the significant other. The child's developing self is engaged in a process of internalising and organising; the significant other is engaged in the process of reflecting and interpreting. We must be in control of this dialogue, ensuring that the messages, both verbal and non-verbal, help a child to feel respected and valued.

HOWEVER...it is not always that straightforward!

"Everyone has inside himself....what shall I call it....a piece of good news. Everyone is a very great and important character. Yes, that's what we have to tell them. Every man must be persuaded, even if he's in rags, that he is immensely, immensely important. Every one must respect him and make him respect himself too. They must listen to him attentively, don't stand on top of him, don't stand in his light, but look at him with gentleness, deference, give him great, great hopes, he needs them, especially if he's young...spoil him. Yes, make him grow proud."

BURNT FLOWER BED   Ugo Betti (an Italian play)

The Interactionist Approach

When talking to children we so often hear them say that adults responsible for their care or education "don't like them, think they are useless, don't listen to them....etc." When we talk to those same adults we generally meet kind and concerned people who are genuinely looking for ways to relate to the kid in their care.

What has caused this misunderstanding? Why is there such a mis-match in the perceptions of the relationship between the two?

The interactionist approach is based on the assumption that the way a person feels about himself determines the way he behaves and the way he interprets the meaning of the behaviour of others towards him.

Mead (1934) presents a framework to explain how we operate as individuals and relate to others. He states that we live in a symbolic world where spoken language and body language convey meaning. People make interpretations from what we say and do. We predict the behaviour of others and gauge our behaviour according to the expectations we believe others have. In every situation we construct a self-concept consistent with the expectations we perceive others to have of us.

The interactionist approach forces us to think, not just about the symbols of interaction, but how the symbols are interpreted. And this includes the interpretation of all aspects of our communication, not just what we say but how we say it! Our non-verbal behaviour contains many important signals:

WE SPEAK WITH OUR TONGUES

WE COMMUNICATE WITH OUR WHOLE BODIES.

Always be aware that the way that you sit or stand, the tone of voice that you use and your gestures contribute to the message that you give:

THE WORDS YOU USE TODAY ARE SOMEONE'S SELF-CONCEPT TOMORROW.

Biased Scanning

Accepting the significance of our interactions with children doesn't tell the whole story. The message we intend to convey is subject to the perceptions of the receiver and children who feel badly about themselves may distort or misinterpret our intentions. BIASED SCANNING is the process by which information which is consistent with the self-concept is eagerly accepted; information inconsistent with self-concept is either ignored, misinterpreted or rejected. Children with low self-concept will look for information to confirm their poor view of themselves. Significant others must constantly offer unambiguous messages of acceptance.

Research

Research is far too important to be left to researchers.

We have chosen a few examples of the research which interested or excited us. Each example describes an intervention which, after reading about it, we felt, "I would like to try that!"

1. Lawrence (1973)

Several pieces of work have looked for an improvement in self-concept after an intervention intended to raise attainment, i.e. "Will he feel better about himself if we teach him to read?" We like Lawrence's approach better; he asks the question "Will he read better if we help him to feel better about himself?" Lawrence offered some brief training to volunteers and they then "counselled" groups of primary school children identified as backward readers. The results showed that the counselling had more effect on reading progress than extra teaching. Our own experience with disturbed children who often also have learning difficulties is that 'extra help' can sometimes confirm a child's feelings of failure and this might work against progress.

Subsequent research has confirmed that any remedial intervention is more likely to be successful if the teacher systematically pays attention to the pupil's self-concept. Lawrence's own recent work carried out in Australia, (Lawrence 1988) examines further and re-confirms the increased effectiveness of teaching interventions when they are combined with programmes or activities which increase the self-concept of the pupils involved.

The popular emphasis on parental involvement in children's reading probably owes its success to the sharing of the positive experience by the parent, the child and the school.

2. Gibby and Gibby (1976)

They arranged for some high achieving students to take some attainment tests and a self-esteem inventory. A week later the students were called back to re-sit the tests but this time half of them were given a slip of paper telling them that they had done badly last time. Guess what this did to their results?.....   RIGHT!   Oh Gibby and Gibby, why didn't you tell some of them that they had done really well? That would have been so much kinder!

3. Hartley (1986)

Robert Hartley starts his piece of work by describing his own situation as a student facing the awful prospect of preparing to re-sit his G.C.E. O-Level examination. Faced with a blank sheet of paper and an equally blank mind he produces an especially good piece of work by imagining that he is a BBC newsreader. When the piece of work comes back with praise from the teacher, Hartley can remember thinking, "Why hadn't they told me they wanted me to be someone else?" In his own research work he then demonstrates that children can significantly improve their performance when they attempt tasks in role as the cleverest pupil in the class. However, when the children go on to discuss their success they disown it as someone else's work...."Somebody else was doing them. I bet when I do them I will get them all wrong!"

5. Clark and Walberg(1968)

Although most people regard praise as something which should be offered generously but not excessively this piece of research showed that 'over the top' can work well under certain conditions. Six classes of 10 to 13 year old children with reading difficulties were offered very frequent praise for a period of three weeks. Each positive comment was recorded by the pupil on a special tally card so that the child retained lasting evidence of the praise. After three weeks three of the teachers were asked to increase the frequency of the praise by a factor of two to three. The other three were just told to keep up the good work. After a further three weeks the most frequently praised group showed a significantly greater improvement in reading attainment than the control group. This may be attributed to:

very frequent praise.

recording of each positive statement.

intervention only lasting for a few weeks.

More work needed but in the meantime: Praise him, Praise him, Praise him!

6. Bevan and Shorthall (1986)

In this experiment four infant teachers were instructed to touch children only when praising good academic or social behaviour. No deliberate increase in praise was attempted. The combined use of touch and praise was found to have a dramatic effect. Children spent 40% more time on task, the number of disruptive incidents decreased and teachers spent less time telling children off.

7. Wheldall and Merrett (1988)

During observations of a large sample of teaching sessions in secondary schools in the West Midlands Wheldall and Merrett observed teachers' use of praise and disapproval. They found that teachers used three times as much praise as disapproval when commenting on academic work but when the comments related to behaviour the ratio was reversed and the negative comments were three times more frequent than the positive ones. They stated that approval for good social behaviour was rarely expressed.

Useful research does not depend on vast data collection exercises, access to huge samples and an army of assistants. Many of the most creative and enlightening pieces of work have been small scale, simple projects. The process of asking your own questions and finding answers which you can use to change the way you work is important and exciting. Reading about other people's work, however good, cannot compare with doing your own.

> *"If research is a product, in the end it is only the experience of production, and access to the means of production, that makes it usable."*

Paley, J. 1980

We have used the quotation from Paley's article to suggest to you that the research we do ourselves, however modest, is more relevant because we participate in finding the answers to the questions we have asked. We and the children in our care benefit from the application of the knowledge that we have gained.

Our Research on Children's Understanding of Language

We followed our own advice and carried out a small scale investigation which is described below.

In our work at Woodstock school the staff seem to have developed a particular style of communication with the children. It includes the use of very simple and clear verbal messages followed by a careful checking of the child's understanding. We thought it likely that this had developed because we have assumed that many of the children have some difficulty in understanding the spoken language we use in everyday conversation.

Our Question – Are we right in that assumption?

This was examined more carefully during the summer of 1987 when we decided to assess the understanding of received language using the Test of Reception of Grammar. (T.R.O.G.) Although our population falls into the normal ability range the testing revealed a significantly skewed set of results, with average scores more than two years below chronological ages and 18% of the children at the 1st percentile. This means that many children will have serious problems when attempting to follow instructions, listen to stories and participate in conversation.

We cannot offer an explanation for the demonstrated association of poor understanding of language and placement in a school for pupils with emotional and behavioural difficulties. If the relationship is causal then more research is needed to establish which is the cause and which the effect. What it has offered is justification for our communication style and for the formation of a special language teaching group.

Don't accept Nod for and Answer

As a result of this piece of work we now place an even greater emphasis on the necessity to use clear language and to check carefully that we have been understood. Asking a child, "Do you understand?" and accepting a nod as confirmation is not sufficient. How can the child who has not understood be sure of that? The failure to understand a small but crucially important part of the message may lead the pupil into a great deal of trouble for which he will have no rational explanation.

Perception Check..

Rather than accepting a nod or a "yes" when you ask a child, "Have you understood?" it may be more helpful to look for other ways to check that your message has been understood or that you both share the same view of your agreement…

"Just to make sure we are both clear can you tell me what we have agreed?"

"Will you explain to me what you are going to do now?"

This sounds friendly and courteous and indicates that you have a shared responsibility for clear communication; not that it is the other person's fault if she has misunderstood.

Taking Ownership

We also believe that when the child talks about an understanding or an intention in her own language then she is taking ownership of the agreement and may well be more likely to carry out stated behaviour than if she is merely the recipient of an instruction.

"I am going to go and tidy up the mess I made in the classroom and then apologise to Mr. Smith."

"I am going to bring my reading book back tomorrow."

Changes in Teacher Talk

In 1988/9 we were able to pursue our interest in the effects of teacher language upon behaviour when Barbara had an opportunity to do some research on the topic.

A group of teachers working with children aged six to eight were asked to make some changes in the language they used in the classroom. These were:

1 Before giving any instruction or information the teacher was asked to pay special attention to maintaining the child's attention by using her name, keeping eye contact.

2 Efforts were made to improve the clarity of the language and avoid classroom jargon and school based codes which might be misunderstood by some children.

3 Check the child's understanding before ending the interaction.

4 Encourage the child to state in her own language the agreed plan or an understanding of the information.

During the research project the frequency of "disruptive behaviours" was measured in a selection of pupils who had been described as difficult to maintain on task and often in trouble. The effects of the changes in teacher language were to reduce by 50% the observed incidents of disruption.

The importance to the pupil of an adequate understanding of the language she hears in school cannot be underestimated since she is likely to be required to understand, learn from or obey teacher talk every few minutes of the school day.

You Work With Children?
You Want Answers?
You Too Can Do Research

A Bag of Tricks

Working with children in trouble and watching other people has given us the opportunity to collect a bag full of ideas, tricks and strategies. Some may seem fun and they are presented in a light-hearted way but they are all based on the principle that children with low self-concept are vulnerable; they need protecting from their own destructive behaviour and they need to be accepted.

Label the Act

Never tell a child he is bad, a liar, a thief. Sure, you are displeased with his BEHAVIOUR, but you still value him. So maintain his self-esteem and tell him that you are disappointed or surprised that a good child like him has done a thing like that. It's just not like him! That way you can both start to expect that he won't do it again.

Money in the Pocket

Children come to you with different levels of self-concept and those with high self-concept are likely to achieve the best results. We can make the comparison with money; those with most money in their pockets can take risks, try new things, afford to risk a little and even if they lose some they are not poor. The child with low self-concept is like a child with very little money. He can't afford to gamble because he runs the risk of failing and being left with nothing at all. So it is up to you to support, encourage and protect the child with low self-concept and you can do this by...

Take the Risk Yourself

When a child faces a task which puts him at risk of failure you can give him courage by taking the responsibility for possible failure onto your own shoulders. For example:

1. Remove the threat of failure: "This is very hard but I know you will do your best. Don't worry if you find it difficult, it is my fault for giving you such hard work."

2. Take the blame for failure: "I am sorry, I didn't explain that properly. It is my fault. Let me try again."

3. Offer just enough help and just early enough to prevent failure and consequent breakdown of concentration. It is much easier to intervene when the child is still on task than to rescue a child with low self-concept once he has failed.

Marking Work

In most of our interactions with children we are close to them, we can observe and react to their response and we can modify our behaviour accordingly. When reprimanding a child for poor work the severity of our message may be softened if the pupil bursts into tears and increased if s/he gazes at the ceiling, shrugs and whistles! When we write comments on the bottom of an exercise book we may not be in the room when the child reads them, we don't know how they are received, whether they are understood, and whether they offer the child any understanding or motivation to improve. What is more we don't know how the child's parents will react when they read the comments at home. Parents can get upset too and if they feel anxious or helpless then they may react unfavourably towards the child. Sometimes children get punished twice: lose their pocket money because they got a detention.

With a little thought it is possible to mark work in a way which encourages a child to improve performance and offers the support and information to enable him to do so. For " You must..." try substituting the words "I will help you to......"

Apologise

During a busy working day it is inevitable that occasionally you might have to keep a child waiting, interrupt your attention to him when you are distracted and maybe not manage to do everything you said you would. Make sure that you say that you are sorry, that you ask if you may keep them waiting whilst you attend to some urgent matter. Offer an explanation for your behaviour. That really makes a child feel important, that you care about him as an individual and that he deserves your respect.

Using Touch

Non-verbal interventions are a very powerful part of the behavioural dialogue. A hand on the shoulder, a pat on the back, a smile can convey to a child that you recognise him as an individual and that you care about him. A brief non-verbal message offered fairly frequently when a child is behaving well can keep a child on task and give a very positive signal.

We will write more extensively about the importance of touch in all educational, work and social settings in a future publication but it is important to make a few points here. Many schools, mainly secondary, and some education authorities are advising or even instructing adults never to touch young people creating alarm and suspicion that they will not be safe to do so. Unfortunately the positive apporach to development of a policy describing and celebrating safe touch seems not to be considered. In a school where touch is forbidden the hall is lined with photographs of the head shaking hands with students on speech day!

Research demonstrates that touch has a very positive effect on emotion and physical well-being and that we use it less in the UK than in any other culture. (Carlson 1994). As well as providing evidence of being 'close', 'in touch', the skin sensation releases powerful chemicals in the brain which regulate the feelings of security and status.

Presumably the advice not to touch is given to reduce the likelihood that accusations of abuse will be made - but isn't it possible that this will have the opposite effect? If we give young people the message that touch is not safe then we raise levels of anxiety and suspicion. Much better to touch frequently, safely, always in public and in association with praise for comfort. It cannot be that this behaviour is safe in other countries but dangerous in the UK.

A Whisper in Time

A very, very quiet word whispered to a child when trouble is brewing can be an effective way of preventing the situation from escalating. It is private, it is non-threatening, it gets the child's attention and it brings you physically close to him. It creates an atmosphere that is calm and quiet and it does not inject emotional energy to which the child may react. (It is also a good way to keep your own blood pressure down!)

Target Teaching to Success

Sometimes our best intended interventions backfire on the child. For example years of remedial teaching might be confirming to the pupil how badly he has failed and for how long. Identifying an agreed goal to work towards, ensuring that the steps to success are small, measurable and can be demonstrated to the child can turn remedial intervention from a spiral of failure into a ladder of success. Ainscow and Tweddle (1979)

Making Punishment Positive

When talking to adults about their own memories of difficult or unhappy situations at school a recurring theme is the sense of injustice. They felt powerless, misunderstood and they weren't able to negotiate a way to put things right. Sometimes this resulted in alienation or a wish to get one's own back and these memories remain with us for years.

I'm not that Strict

After discussing the situation with the pupil and reaching an agreement that the behaviour must be punished in some way, ask the child to suggest an appropriate punishment. Often he will come up with something far more severe than is really needed. This allows you to say something positive and suggest something less strict. The child will leave feeling that you have been fair to him.

Bin it

You may decide that, having obtained the child's agreement that things were not right, no further action is really necessary. A 'symbolic punishment' may be written on a piece of paper and a course of action planned which will allow the pupil to put matters right, (complete his work, apologise to an injured party, clear up a mess...) If the pupil succeeds in this task then the punishment need never be implemented and the child can tear up the piece of paper on which it was written and throw it in the bin!

Don't Feed the Monster

A quiet, non-threatening response to an angry pupil who is out of control often works better than confrontation or a show of greater strength. If you shout back at a pupil who is shouting at you then you may fuel their anger and the initial incident gets forgotten in the escalating situation. Stay calm and quiet, try leaving the room for a minute. Explain that you have to deliver an urgent message and you will return in a moment. When you come back apologise for having been away. If you are lucky then the child will have been surprised by this action and will have calmed down whilst you have avoided a stressful confrontation. If it doesn't work then you have lost nothing and can still use your anger if necessary. Always start with a low level intervention and move up if necessary. It is easier than trying to go in the other direction.

Comment

These ideas are intended to be suggestions rather than prescriptions and you will not necessarily want to use all of them or use them in the way that we describe. It is important that you feel comfortable with the strategies that suit you.

We hope that, more important than the individual ideas, we have conveyed a positive approach and stimulated you to generate, within your own environment, an ethos which supports the management of children's difficult behaviour whilst maintaining good relationships with them. Pupils will not always behave and perform in the ways that we wish or expect. It is only your imagination which limits the number of ways in which you can turn potentially difficult encounters into positive interactions. The important thing is that you work them out for your school and make them your own.

Communication

Clear Sending of Messages

High quality communication depends upon clear sending so that the message that we give is received and understood in the way that we had intended. The better we are able disclose about the way we really feel the more effective our communication will be.

These self-disclosing messages are called 'I' messages as opposed to the alternative 'You' messages that we often use. 'You' messages talk about and often judge the behaviour of others such as,

> "You are all ignoring me."

An appropriate "I" message alternative might be:

> "I feel left out."

Positive 'I' Messages

Many of the positive messages we give to others are judgemental,

> "That is a good piece of work."

> "You are very good at swimming."

Praise is important and many children will accept these statements as confirmation of their own view of their work or athletic prowess. However we are more often looking for opportunities to give approbation to the majority who produce average work or who may make an effort even if the end results cannot be described as 'good' This was made clear to us when the judgemental praise so often seemed ineffective or was clearly rejected by the receiver. A child told that her painting is very good may mutter, "It's rubbish" or even tear it up if she has not achieved the result that she judges to be good. Try a positive 'I' message:

> "You have used lovely bright colours... this picture makes me feel really cheerful."

Because you have included an expression of your feelings the message is less likely to be rejected and includes a really personal, positive message.

Positive 'I' messages are not just for pupils and by expressing your true feelings the messages you send are more likely to be effective in any relationship. There is no trick or special skill... just say what you feel.

Activity

Think of a positive 'I' message that you would like to send to someone in your life, a member of your family. a colleague or a young person.

Write the message in a particular way:

"When you... (decribe the behaviour)

> I feel..."

Make sure that you use a genuine emotion and underline the 'feeling' word.

When you text me for no particular reason I feel valuable to you and loved.

Confrontive "I" Language

'I' Language is not limited to the situations when we wish to give praise or positive messages. It can be used very effectively when you want to change someone's behaviour. Often when someone is behaving in a way which causes us a problem we send a 'You' message.

For example many of the messages we send to children are 'YOU' messages;

YOU... "Sit down and shut up!"

YOU... "Be quiet or else!"

YOU... "always start trouble!"

These messages either warn or blame. They imply that the pupil has the problem and pupils with low self-concept will accept this as a confirmation of their own opinion of themselves. The impact of the message relies on the teacher's authority and is therefore vulnerable to confrontation, one winner and one loser. Notice how easy it is to shout when delivering a "YOU" message.

Activity

Think of a time when someone has behaved in a way that has had a bad effect on you and remember the way you spoke when angry or upset... Write down the actual words you used.

You lot don't deserve to have all these new footballs!.

An alternative is a CONFRONTIVE "I" MESSAGE where the adult communicates his FEELINGS and allows the pupil to respond by being considerate, helpful and kind. It is less likely to provoke an angry response and reduces conflict; e.g. for "(YOU) Be Quiet!" say "I get frustrated by all this noise."

We may be reluctant to expose our feelings to the children but when we do it often produces unexpectedly positive responses.

What's in a Three Part Confrontive "I" Message?

The BEHAVIOUR, e.g. shouting out.

The EFFECT, e.g. stopping me finishing the story.

The FEELINGS, e.g. I get irritated.

"When you shout out it stops me finishing the story and I feel irritated."

An "I" message might not always include all three aspects but they are implicit and convey that you are a real person. Your distress is blamed on the effect of the behaviour and not on the pupil. For this reason it is more likely to be spoken in a moderate voice. A good "I" message acknowledges a problem and opens the way to the search for a solution without allocating blame and provoking conflict.

Advantages of "I" Messages

Communicates feelings.

Reduces the likelihood of confrontation.

Opens up possibility of discussion.

Protects the self-concept of the pupil.

Allows the adult to stay calm and express feelings.

Warning

Sometimes the effectiveness of an "I" message is reduced because the real feelings are not communicated. For example, imagine a group of children working reasonably well, on task, but accompanied by a high level of chatter and general classroom noise. To a teacher working in an empty corridor this might be quite acceptable but we have all experienced the disapproval of colleagues who have been disturbed by the noise from our pupils.

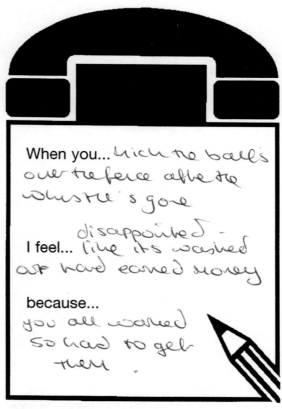

When you... kick the balls over the fence after the whistle's gone

I feel... disappointed - like its washed out hard earned money

because... you all worked so had to get them.

We may have said, "I am getting very angry because there is too much noise." Superficially this may appear to be an 'I' message but it really conveys a secondary feeling and does not open the door to solving the real problem. Our anger is a consequence of our feelings of embarrassment or inadequacy because of the impression our noisy class may make on the teachers nearby. If we communicate this feeling accurately to the children then we are less likely to spoil the good working atmosphere. It also offers more the possibility of better solutions, e.g. asking the teachers nearby whether they are being disturbed, and if so working out with the pupils how this can be reduced or avoided.

So why don't you try a confrontive 'I' message sometime soon. If it fails then you can always shout a 'YOU' message later! If it works well then try the six steps to finding a solution as described on page 19:

Dos and Don'ts

We often give an instruction by describing the behaviour we don't want... "Don't run!", "Don't drop that cup!", "Don't hit Mary!" The brain cannot create an image of a "Don't' so it is much better to describe the behavour we do want... "Walk carefully!", "Hold the cup safely!", "Play gently with Mary so that you are both safe!"

Activity

Rewrite one of your frequent 'Don't..'. messages into a positive alternative.

Listening

When we send a confrontive 'I' message it will not necessarily result in an immediate response; often it will be met by resistance. If we send again we run the high risk of strengthening this resistance and escalating the conflict.

For example:

"When you leave your wet clothes on the radiator it makes a horrible smell and I feel uncomfortable," may be answered by, "What do you expect me to do then... go home soaking wet?"

If we go on to say,

"Don't you speak to me like that... I don't like the wet clothes on the radiator," the feelings between the two parties have been made worse.

It is important to hear, recognise and accept that the other person has some strong feelings and if we can make that clear we are more likely to get a positive response. An appropriate response to the resistance could have been,

"You think that I don't care about you going home in wet clothes."

This technique is called SHIFTING GEARS and it involves alternating between sending confrontive "I" messages and listening to the resistance so that the energy of anger is taken away from the interaction whilst you continue to state your feelings and ask for the behaviour to change. The student might not easily change right away but shifting gears can lead up to the point at which you can say something like,

"It seems to me we both have a problem. You need to get your things dry and I don't want the room to smell of damp clothes. Let's see if we can look for a solution which makes us both happy."

This sets the stage for a lead into the six step problem solving process described on page 19.

Listening when a Student has a Problem

Sometimes it may be that the student has the problem and the need for change is not coming from the teacher. He may however notice some signs that there is a problem and can make matters worse by ignoring or not listening. It is sometimes easier and quicker to use roadblocks such as asking probing questions, offering solutions or expressing sympathy rather than to really listening to what is coming from the student.

An example from one of our workshops illustrates the point. An infant teacher told about a girl who often came into class upset, crying and clearly unhappy. She had used a variety of techniques:

"What is the matter with you today?"   - questioning

"You poor thing" and a cuddle   - sympathy

"Go and sit in the book corner until you feel better."   - solution

Nothing seemed to make any difference until she tried listening and giving some space for a response. Her opening words were,

"You are feeling really sad and unhappy today" - "listening" to behaviour and checking feelings.

The girl responded by sitting on the teacher's knee and starting to talk about her unhappiness. It might not always work so quickly but if we can actively listen by checking out how the other person is feeling and leaving the door open for time to talk the communication will be improved.

The Six Step Problem Solving Method
...which has seven steps!

0. Setting the Stage

Before you can begin to problem solve you must show that you have listened, understood and that you have the other person's agreement to go ahead and help her find her own solution.

1. Defining the Problem

It is very important that the pupils understand from the very beginning that this is not just a gimmick but a serious attempt to find a way to reduce an area of conflict by involving everybody. Show that the process is important by allocating time and by listening carefully and taking every contribution seriously. Be sure to state your feelings, give "I" messages.

2. Generate Possible Solutions

Collect all ideas without any evaluation or judgement at this stage and display them where everyone can see them. Encourage all contributions.

3. Evaluate the Solutions

Take time to gather a wide range of positive and negative views about the ideas on the list. Make your own feelings explicit and delete from the list any solution which is unacceptable to you or to the group as a whole.

4. Choosing a Solution

You are looking for a solution which will satisfy everybody by negotiation and consensus, not simply the most popular choice by vote which may leave a significant number of pupils very dissatisfied. Support pupils in expressing a minority viewpoint. The eventual solution may not be anyone's first choice but should be fairly well up everybody's list.

5. Decide how to Implement the Solution

Identify the conditions, allocate the responsibilities and agree standards of success, e.g. "When is soon?", "How clean is clean?", "What do we mean by rude?", "How loud is shouting?" It is often a good idea to put up the solution agenda for continuing reference.

6. Assessing the Success of the Solution

Discuss changes which have taken place, reasons for success and failure and identify any unexpected difficulties. If necessary... start again!

(Summarised from *Teacher Effectiveness Training* by Thomas Gordon)

What is Emotional Literacy?

Emotional Literacy - or emotional intelligence, as it is sometimes called, is the ability to recognise, understand, handle and appropriately express emotions - both your own, and those of others.

Children and adults who are emotionally literate are able to get on with others, resolve conflicts, motivate themselves and achieve in life.

We hear a lot about the importance of 'ordinary' literacy, numeracy, and other key skills. We often assume that it is the presence or absence of these skills and the amount of 'ordinary' intelligence a child or adult has, which determines how successful they will be.

But there is a great deal of evidence to show that this is not actually so. Emotional literacy, or emotional intelligence, is actually a better predictor of lifelong achievement than is conventional IQ. A person's IQ predicts only a small part of lifelong success - ranging from 4 to 20 per cent. Emotional intelligence, on the other hand, predicts about 80% of a person's success in life.

If we look at children in school, we can see why this might be so. To succeed in today's curriculum, children need to be able to work with others, to be aware of others' perspectives, and sensitive to their feelings. They need to be able to communicate effectively, be good listeners, learn how to be clear about their own wants and needs and learn how to resolve differences. They need to be able to motivate themselves, persevere at tasks, avoid seeking instant gratification. They need to be able to manage themselves, which means understanding and managing what they are feeling at any given time.

The importance of emotional intelligence has obvious implications for education. It is no longer enough to develop conventional, rational thinking skills in the classroom. We need to consider 'educating differently' so as to develop children's multiple intelligences, rather than focusing exclusively on a narrow range of skills.

Five good reasons for teaching Emotional Literacy

As we have seen, the first good reason for teaching emotional literacy is that it will help children to achieve in their school work, and help schools break through the statistics to achieve the demanding targets that are set by and for them.

The second good reason is that it will enable children to continue to succeed when they leave school: to hold down jobs, to sustain relationships, to contribute to society, to become lifelong learners.

The third reason is that teaching emotional literacy will promote mental health - particularly important at a time when we know that mental health problems are increasing at an alarming rate, especially amongst children.

The fourth reason is that it will make teaching easier. Where schools have put an emotional literacy programme in place, they have found that the school becomes a more harmonious place. There are fewer tensions, fewer quarrels, less aggression. Children are more task-focused and adults spend less time sorting out problems and more time teaching.

The final reason for teaching emotional literacy is about promoting understanding and tolerance in schools and in society. Children who have learned to understand others' feelings are less likely to be drawn into discrimination or bullying. They are less likely to join in with the hatreds that set group against group, more likely to be valued peacemakers, problem-solvers, and friends.

How emotional literacy develops

Conventional literacy has its word level skills, sentence level skills, and text level skills - all developing at their own rate from limited beginnings in early childhood to the sophisticated skills of the mature reader/writer.

Emotional literacy also has its separate skills, which develop over time. These are:

The skill of recognising, naming and describing feelings - developing from the baby's crude non-verbal expression of two or three emotions, through to the mature adult's ability to recognise and name a wide range of different feelings.

The capacity for understanding others' feelings, or empathy - developing from the small child's smile at another's pleasure to the ability of some adults to pick up very subtle clues from others, to ' feel for' them, and to empathise in relation to imagined situations, outside the here and now.

The ability to manage one's own feelings - developing from being totally overwhelmed by them in infancy and early childhood, to the later ability to control and channel anger, consciously reduce anxiety, or reframe situations mentally so as to alter the emotions they produce.

The skills of communication - becoming able to talk about feelings, becoming a good listener, learning about negotiation and confl ict resolution.

The ability to set goals and solve problems - developing from the young child's immediate goals and inability to wait, through to a mature capacity to evaluate different solutions to problems, and plan for the long term rather than ' now'.

The grid on pages 22-23 shows in more detail how emotional literacy develops from birth to maturity. Not all of us - children and adults alike - succeed in reaching the more sophisticated levels of emotional literacy, just as not all children become conventionally literate as adults.

Nevertheless the grid gives us an idea of where teaching emotional literacy is aiming. It can be used by schools as a planning tool for developing their own emotional curriculum, which will take children through the key skills, introducing them in the early years of schooling then re-visiting them cyclically as children grow and develop.

How can we find the time?

Many schools are already teaching parts of the emotional curriculum, through Circle Time, drama, story, assemblies, personal and social education ' lessons' and any number of other formal and informal ways of promoting thinking about feelings.

Emotional literacy is more complex than this, and more pervasive. It can be learned when a teacher stops reading a shared text in the conventional literacy hour, to ask how a certain character might be feeling, and what might happen next. It can be learned when a teacher stops two fourteen year olds fighting, and asks each of them to listen while the other gives their reasons for the conflict, and what they want to get from a solution. It is learning which can take place in a wide range of situations, throughout the school day.

Things that are meant to happen everywhere, however, can sometimes end up happening nowhere. Things that should pervade the curriculum can simply get lost.

What we are suggesting is that schools do give priority to this area as part of their thinking on personal, health and social education and citizenship. We are also suggesting that they develop systems for mapping the emotional literacy skills they want to develop, in each year group and class, and for planning how they will address these skills through the ways that fit best for them.

This might be a weekly assembly at the start of the week, where a theme is introduced which each class takes up during the week, producing work to share at assembly on Friday.

It might be through the use of regular circle time throughout the school, with Circle Time activities planned so that there is progression and so that all the key skills of emotional literacy are covered. It might be through a secondary PSHE programme, backed up by work in drama in all year groups.

Emotional Literacy –

Talking About Feelings	Listening Skills	Self-awareness
Non-verbal expression of feelings - crying, laughing.	Earliest signals - eye contact, attention, turn head.	Experiencing pleasure, discomfort or pain.
Expressing need "want", desire "no".	Following simple instruction.	Having sad, cross, happy feelings.
	Listening to story - extended attention.	
	Turn taking in conversation.	
Acknowledging "I feel sad," "I feel happy" to adult prompt.		
Acknowledging more complex feelings after adult prompting.	Can encourage other person to talk and use eye contact, body language etc.	
Being able to separate the facts of an event (fight etc.) from the feelings.	Listen to story, answer questions about content.	Thinking about feelings.
Recognising and describing own feelings in specific situations. Developing emotional vocabulary for describing own feelings (e.g: I feel worried, scared, pleased) and for gradations of feelings (a bit scared, very scared).		Understanding the natural and normal range of feelings experienced after a major event such as bereavement/loss.
Using vocabulary of more subtle emotions e.g: embarrassment, shame, anxiety, jealousy.	Reflecting back feelings/content of spoken information.	
Knowing when it is appropriate to talk about feelings and when it is not.	Inferring meaning, predicting, hypothesising. Reflecting back in simple ways the unspoken feelings behind what another person is saying.	Understanding the relationship between thoughts, feeling and actions.
Using 'I' messages (When you do x I feel y, and the consequences are z) to verbalise feelings without blame and to give positive strokes to others.	Using "You feel ... because" when listening. Not being afraid of silence. Being able to follow/summarise content and feeling of what others have said.	Knowing if a thought or feeling is ruling a decision, and being able to identify that thought or that feeling.
Using conflict management skills.	Using conflict management skills.	Knowing whether a feeling/ behaviour is coming from an internal child, adult or parent position.

**Developed by Bristol Teachers and Psychologists
Reprinted from 'The Emotional Literacy Hour, Lucky Duck Publishing Ltd**

a Developmental Progression

Managing Feelings	Empathy	Goal-setting and Planning – Problem-solving and Decision-making
	Simple reflex response to others' emotions e.g: smile at another's pleasure, cry if see someone hurt.	Goals are immediate and waiting impossible.
Knowing that it is OK to have both positive and negative feelings.	Simple acts based on what would make themselves better e.g.: giving another child their comfort object to hold. Early sharing (I will share because they have not got any).	Beginning to be aware of a time scale beyond the here and now, and to be able to predict events. Can set short-term goals with adult help (e.g: High Scope). Can imagine good things to come and tolerate waiting/turntaking. Can set and describe short-term goals without help.
Developing ways of managing your own feelings e.g: asking for help, saying how you feel. Being able to receive and respond to others' strong emotions.	Simple perspective taking e.g: answering questions about a story - "How do you think Brown Bear is feeling?"	Can set and describe longer term goals, and begin to make informed choices between "now" and "later". Can generate alternative solutions to social/interpersonal problems and begin to identify consequence of doing x, y, or z.
Developing more complex ways of managing feelings, e.g: assertiveness, visualisation, relaxation, changing the way you internally talk to yourself and perceive/label events.	More complex clue reading to deduce others' feelings - simple feelings of pleasure, anger, sadness. Can pick up others' very subtle emotions - embarrassment, jealousy, shame etc. Multiple perspective taking - seeing everybody's side of things. Can maintain empathy beyond the here and now. Ability to empathise in relation to imagined situations outside own experience. Ability to manage and channel empathy; maintain boundary between self and others; choose whether or not to make a response as a result of empathic feelings.	Can take responsibility for own actions and understand their effects on others. Can plan intermediate steps towards a goal. Can identify a range of solutions to social/ interpersonal problems, examine the probable consequences of each. and make a choice on the basis of this evaluation. Review choices made to see if they worked out. Able to postpone gratification for the sake of others - and work to intrinsic goals.
Managing Feelings	Empathy	Goal-setting and Planning – Problem-solving and Decision-making

The important thing is that the emotional curriculum does not become another straitjacket. It is intended as a framework which teachers can use to decide where they want to get to. How they then get there will be their decision.

How do young people acquire emotional literacy?

The MOT Theory

Model   Do we model the behavours we expect

Opportunity Do we provide the means for pupils to practise and acquire the skills (such as Circle Time)?

Teach   Most young people acquire these skills by modeling, opportunity and practice. These are such important skills, they should not be left to chance, and we should be teaching an emotional curriculum.

At the end of a training session on Anger Management I collected up the evaluation forms and looked through them. It had been a busy, active afternoon with a very large group of teachers. To get the attention of the whole group at the end of an activity I had used the raised hand signal... "Hands up, jaws up!" Two participants sitting together had complained that this was "patronising - we do this to the children." I was genuinely shocked. How could anyone think that is is acceptable to behave towards children in ways that are not aceptable for us? if we are not prepared to model politeness and courtesy then how can this whole process begin?

Circle Time

The meaning of circles

Individuals meet to form societies which perform a variety of functions. The purpose of these meetings might be understood by observing the physical formation of the individuals in the group. A naive observer would recognise a view of parliament as an adversarial contest between opposing participants. She would also recognise a court room scene as the imposition of power by high status individuals upon a deviant or rejected member. A discussion held in circular formation or a dance in the round would probably be interpreted as co-operative and non-hierarchical. The image of North American indigents passing the peace pipe around a circle, the link-armed singing of Auld Lang Sine in a circle or even the preparation for war in a circular dance convey a unified purpose shared by all members of the group.

Developing the ideas

If you are reading this book it is likely that you already have some experience through reading or participation in Circle groups. In the publication *Circle Time* by Teresa Bliss and Jo Tetley (1993) we described the structure, rules and activities which form the basis of starting and maintaining Circle Time groups. These are only briefly referred to in this publication. It is not until you start to use the processes for yourself that you will discover the fun and the deeper values achieved in Circle Time. In order to convey this more vividly we made a training video called *Coming Round to Circle Time* (1995). If you have seen this video then you will already be aware of our commitment to and our enthusiasm for Circle Time as an important contribution to the development of altruistic and empathic behaviours, vital to any civilised and peaceful society. In this publication we hope to offer Circle Time enthusiasts some more ideas about extending their work and to answer some of the questions which have arisen in discussion groups.

Circle Time has two main components: content and process. Our first publication dealt mainly with the former and in this one we will put an emphasis on process. As a facilitator you will already have developed your own style and your group will have favourite games and activities. We hope that this publication will help you to increase the value of something that is already rewarding and enjoyable.

Circle Time is now quite likely to be found in British schools as a regular activity for pupils. Justification of the use of precious class time can be established by relating the various activities to National Curriculum targets.

The value of Circle Time lies in the possibility for development and acceptance for the participants rather than in a goal oriented process of problem solving. Because it is easy to begin Circle Time and because it is fun for all those involved, it may be that some users do not consider the values and assumptions that underpin the process. Ballard (1982) identifies ten value statements and suggests that if teachers do not share these they will have difficulty in conducting Circle Time. Whilst not wishing to be as restrictive as Ballard we would ask the reader to consider the beliefs listed below and their intrinsic relationship with the concept of Circle Time.

Our beliefs

* Children are essentially good if they are treated with respect.

* Teachers are in a powerful position, responsible for the environment within which children learn.

* This environment should be supportive and accepting if it is to foster the best development of young people.

* Teachers should be thoughtful about their position of power in relation to pupils and

should avoid using fear to control behaviour. Fear does not enable and it cannot encourage the development of self-motivated young people.

* Teachers' expectations of the ability and worth of a young person are inevitably transmitted and these expectations will affect the self-image of the young person. The teacher, therefore, has a responsibility to convey acceptance and encouragement.

* If young people are to become self-reliant adults they must be given the opportunity to make choices and the responsibility for the consequences of those choices.

* The ability to make a good decision is dependent on knowledge of self and knowledge of others. In order to achieve this awareness it is important to be able to identify needs of self and needs of the other person and to understand the conflict that may arise in a relationship where these needs are not congruent.

* Understanding of needs and resolution of conflicts depends upon two essential skills: the ability to listen when other people speak and the ability to speak clearly about one's own feelings.

What happens in Circle Time?

The process of Circle Time involves the key skills required by any individual belonging to a social group. Ballard (1982) describes Circle Time as:

1. Awareness - knowing who I am.

2. Mastery - knowing what I can do.

3. Social interaction - knowing how I function in the world of others.

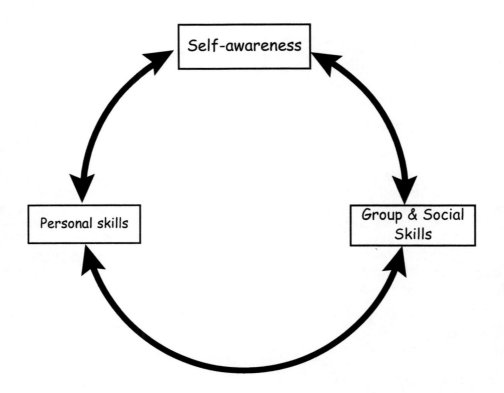

Circle Time is an inter-related, interactive, multi-layered process. Within the Circle participants learn about self, learn about others and relate this knowledge to build relationships between individuals and between groups. The aims for self are to:

* communicate needs

* understand the needs of others

* increase confidence, raise self-esteem.

The N.C.C. (1993) publication on spiritual and moral development points out the essential requirements for the development of young people as:

> "*Self knowledge, relationships, feelings and emotions are an essential part of the spiritual and moral development of young people.*
>
> *Self knowledge. An awareness of oneself in terms of thoughts, feelings, emotions, responsibilities and experiences; a growing understanding and acceptance of individual identity; the development of self-respect.*
>
> *Relationships. Recognising and valuing the worth of each individual; developing a sense of community; the ability to build up relationships with others.*
>
> *Feelings and Emotions. The sense of being moved by beauty or kindness; hurt by injustice or aggression; a growing awareness of when it is important to control emotions and feelings, and how to learn to use such feelings as a source of growth.*"

(page 3)

These three essential elements from the N.C.C. document can link the skills represented in the first diagram.

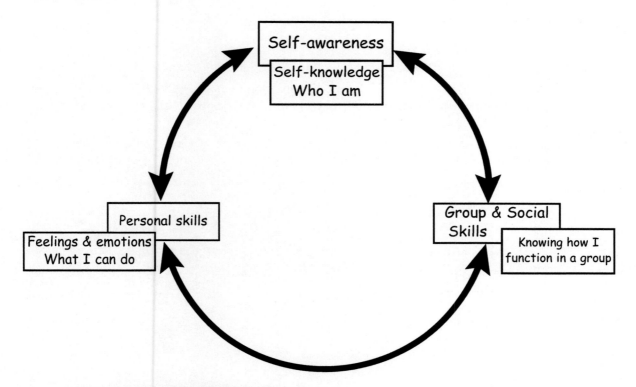

Self-awareness : Self-knowledge: Who I am

Circle Time helps young people to become aware of themselves. Until we learn about ourselves we cannot learn about other people. Some of the activities in Circle Time achieve this by encouraging young people to make "I" statements, I like....., I feel..... These are personal statements about self, the rules of Circle Time demand that the group give acceptance to their "I" statements and that they can therefore be made in safety. Whilst one person is making a personal statement the other group members are learning:

* to listen to other people

* to avoid put-downs and negative statements

* to respect the need for confidentiality and the boundaries of space and time around the group

Circle Time provides consent and permission for young people to talk about feelings and emotions, joy and sadness, pain and pleasure. The participants learn about their own feelings and about the feelings of others. They also learn how to express them verbally and non-verbally. The relationships between needs, behaviour and feelings can be explored and these may be focused on particular themes such as friendship, co-operation, loss or conflict. For example,

"When I fall out with a friend I feel......" "The best day I ever had was ...."

Ballard (1982) identifies four ways in which Circle Time helps to develop and provides an opportunity to communicate self-understanding and self-awareness.

1. Focusing on a particular topic or statement and understanding its implications.

2. Hearing other people's contributions and comparing them with our own perspectives.

3. Learning to disclose openly only what is comfortable to communicate at that time.

4. To receive feedback by watching and listening to the responses of the group and learning from this feedback.

These processes of open communication and acceptance help the individual participant to reduce the natural and cultural inhibitions we often experience when discussing strong emotions.

Self-disclosure

Self-disclosure about feelings, assumptions and beliefs will enable others in the group to have access and therefore insight into the private world of other members. It is a crucial activity within the group and essential for its growth.

The self-disclosure encouraged needs to be kept at a safe level. It is best to start with simple statements such as favourites, e.g.:

TV. programmes

foods

music.

Even these may be hard for some people. The group's reaction to the disclosure will establish the safety to allow progress to more sensitive information, e.g.:

falling out with a friend

getting bullied

or even:

feeling shy

living in a one-parent family.

If a young person discloses the name of a favourite pop group and this is greeted with shrieks of derision then the message is sent that it is not safe to express this view. This will limit the group's opportunity to grow because there will be a taboo on certain subjects or a rejection of certain individuals. The participants fail to function as a unified group because of:

a lack of trust

a lack of support and care offered.

Self-disclosure needs to take place at a pace that is appropriate for the group because the reaction of the group will determine the level and extent of genuine disclosures possible in the future. Groups that are mature enough to offer unconditional acceptance will give total support and love to individual members. It is our experience that this can be achieved by young people who are used to the ethos of Circle Time. It is important to remember that self-disclosure is not just about words - tone of voice and facial expression might indicate that very strong emotions accompany quite neutral words e.g. I don't like playtime. There are three important issues that are relevant to self-disclosure.

Group and social skills: Relationships: Knowing how I function in a group

As participants become more confident as speakers and listeners they will have opportunities to observe and understand that communication is powerful and underpins process and social function. In pair and group activities young people can experience the effects of what is said on others. This can be learned from experience as an observer, a receiver or a sender of communication within the group. One group asked a particular boy to leave the room and in his absence they made a list of positive statements about him. He was not popular and some young people had to think hard to find something nice to say. They all managed it. When he returned the list was read out to him. He was pleased and said that he particularly liked the comment made by a girl, "He is good at football. "That evening the girl told her mother that she felt much more positively about this boy because he chose her comment as his favourite. The activity had produced reciprocal good feelings as receiving and sending roles were exchanged.

Quite young children can begin to understand their responsibility for the effects of what they say and its significance for friendships, co-operation and conflict resolution. During the life of a circle group this process explored through completion statements might progress from safe examples such as; "A friend is......" "I feel upset when......" to statements which explore personal and group dynamics such as, "Somebody felt sorry for me when......" "The time I did something that others didn't like was......" "The time I made somebody angry was........"

Personal Skills : Feelings and emotions : What can I do?

When one person attempts to convey an idea, an explanation or meaning to another she has in her mind a myriad of facts, feelings and detail. This information is translated and delivered to the other in the form of words, body language, facial expression, tone of voice and gesture. The receiver understands it only in the context of her knowledge of the sender, her experiences and her personal experience of language. The chance that this process achieves 100% accurate shared understanding of meaning is infinitely small.

When the content of the message is factual there is a greater chance that it can be accurately conveyed..." I have brought your book back." When feelings are communicated both the expression and understanding are more difficult and more susceptible to misunderstandings..." I hate parties."

Whilst it is important to convey both facts and feelings we often find in a particularly British use of language, a confusion between these two aspects of language. For example you might hear one person say to another, "I felt you didn't support me at the meeting last night." In this sentence the speaker is not expressing a feeling but a cognitive thought. The sentence might more accurately be expressed as, "I think or know that you did not support me at the meeting last night and I felt upset or irritated."

In Circle Time young people become used to expressing genuine feelings and extend the vocabulary they commonly use for this purpose. The process of expressing and understanding the meaning of any communication is the most vital skill that any of us require as we become effective communicators. Circle Time provides the ideal opportunity to learn these skills, to practise them in a safe environment and to model the skills we have to other learners.

Non-verbal communication

Non-verbal communication as with verbal communication is a skill that can be developed. One of the features of the Circle is the way the group members listen. As one person is speaking the rest of the Circle will be not only listening but usually everybody is looking at the speaker. Pupils will improve their skills in observing body language, facial expressions and voice intonation.

Some of the early activities such as Passing the Squeeze or Passing the Smile can assist the pupils to learn to look into somebody's face or hold somebody's hand without embarrassment.

Self-esteem

Self-esteem has been a focus in much of our work. We believe that pupils who have a positive view of themselves are more likely to achieve more, both socially and academically, than those pupils whose self-esteem is low. Self-esteem seems to be a pre-requisite for a self-disciplined and self-motivated person. The process of Circle Time allows the young person to learn more about herself and move away from an egocentric position. From this self-knowledge comes the ability to recognise the needs of others.

We accept that there are several significant others in the pupils' lives, and some of the class members may come from less than encouraging and supportive home backgrounds. The teacher must accept that she still has an important role to play. Aspects of self-esteem are situationally specific and the total environment of the school, and not just Circle Time, should be planned to demonstrate to all pupils that they are unique, acceptable, cared for and valued.

Summary

Circle Time is a very powerful and enjoyable process that assists both the development of the individual and the individual as a member of the group. The diagram indicates in a circular way the various elements of the inter-related processes.

1. Circle Time should generate a sense of belonging which promotes acceptance and support within the community of the class and school.

2. Circle Time facilitates the growth of self-esteem through public acknowledgement and acceptance of individuals as well as through public celebrations of abilities and achievements.

3. Circle Time encourages the use of a variety of inter-personal skills, listening to others and accepting different viewpoints. This demands the development of cognitive and social competence resulting in both individual and group maturation.

4. Circle Time is enjoyed even by the most difficult pupils. It generates positive peer pressure for behaviour which helps the group to function more effectively.

5. Circle Time allows the forum to explore negative and destructive feelings with the opportunity for peers to provide positive help and support to one another.

6. Circle Time facilitates understanding of individual group members through insights gained during the process. This broadens their perspectives and opens up their knowledge of alternative views on life by making them aware of the variety of experiences, strategies and beliefs people bring to everyday life.

Circle Time may eventually offer a group a framework for addressing problems. However, it should not be confused with Quality Circles. These originated in Japanese industry and are a specific technique for problem solving.

Case Studies

Hareclive Primary School – Mediation

The Context

This extract forms part of a PHSE programme for Year 5/6 pupils. As part of this programme the pupils are trained in Peer Mediation by a teacher from the LEA's Emotional and Behavioural Difficulties Service or a trainer from Bristol Mediation Service. The training involves skills such as listening, giving 'I' messages, and following a structured process for resolving difficulties between two people. The pupils also have regular Circle Time activities.

The Lesson/Activity

In this activity the focus was on conflict and cooperation. The children discuss a variety of pictures in pairs. They describe the events in the photographs and discuss how the people in them might be feeling. They brainstorm words about feelings, play Trust Games and finally role-play and problem-solve a conflict.

The Teacher's Views

It is very empowering for children to have the tools to sort things out for themselves. Children with emotional and behavioural difficulties respond really well to being taught these skills. Given the chance they are able to say how they feel and also learn to listen to each other.

The key is knowing that they will get a turn to speak and don't have to compete for attention. Mediation and conflict resolution are useful life-skills for children to learn and to be helped to practise in supported situations.

What the Children Say

> "*I did a mediation for my mum and dad last night Miss.*"

> "*The infants keep pretending they've got a problem just to get a mediation.*"

> "*I like our mediation training - it helps us to sort out our problems.*"

Outcomes

This session was planned for children to:

- identify a range of conflict situations
- identify the feelings attached to conflict
- practise asking people how they feel and tell them how you feel
- problem solve and reach an acceptable resolution.

The Emotional Literacy Skills Developed in the Activity

These were:

- listening, sharing and turn-taking
- identifying feelings by developing appropriate vocabulary
- owning and reflecting feelings
- negotiating skills.

Using the Activity in Different Contexts for Developing Emotional Literacy

This activity has been used in the following ways:

- teaching Year 5/6 mediation skills to pupils with special needs in a Circle Time format

- training two parallel classes Year 5/6 to become playground mediators
- planning a short mediation programme for a playground squad in large primary schools.

Pen Park School – Locus of Control

The Context

The school in which this activity took place is an 11-16 comprehensive serving an outer city housing estate with significant social deprivation.

The activity forms part of a 'School Survival' programme developed for a group of Year 8 pupils who were experiencing significant difficulty in conforming to school expectations of behaviour. All students were at risk of permanent exclusion from school. The rationale for the course was that the students were not making appropriate choices about their behaviour because they lacked knowledge about how to get themselves out of difficult situations without, as they perceived it, losing face. They were also lacking in the skills and confidence to apply the knowledge once they had acquired it. This course attempted to teach them the behaviours which would help them reduce the risk of exclusion. The course was devised and delivered by the School's Behaviour Coordinator.

The Activity

The extract you have seen shows the group learning about the concept of locus of control. The students have been taught that individuals who have an external locus of control rely on other people or events (often a sanction or reward programme) to determine their behaviours, while individuals with an internal locus of control attribute their success or failure to themselves and their own efforts (or lack of it) and thus take responsibility for their own actions. This is a consolidation activity where the students have to identify whether a situation demonstrates internal or external control.

What the Students Said

"The course helped me stay in school. It got me out of trouble."

"I'm the only person who can change my behaviour. I don't want to be excluded and the course has taught me how to control the way I talk to teachers."

Conclusion

We hope that you will remember that every interaction you have with a child, verbal messages and body language, will be interpreted by him as an evaluation of himself, will affect his self-concept and will thus change him. We are asking you to do everything that you can to make sure that the messages he receives will improve his self-concept.

We don't pretend that this approach will solve all problems for all children. For some it may only touch the surface and there are factors outside your control: the time they spend away from you in the care of other adults, their past experiences and sometimes their physical attributes, may undermine the approach you attempt. Even if you are fighting a losing battle you may be able to do some little thing, to put a small coin in the child's self-concept pocket which he may keep and spend at some time in the future!

> *Liza. "You see, really and truly, apart from the things anyone can pick up, (the dressing and the proper way of speaking, and so on), the difference between a lady and a flower girl is not how she behaves, BUT HOW SHE IS TREATED. I shall always be a flower girl to Professor Higgins, because he always treats me as a flower girl, and always will; but I know I can be a lady to you, because you always treat me as a lady, and always will."*
>
> Pygmalion, George Bernard Shaw.

Our intention has not been to provide you with answers; only you can do that, working in and knowing your own unique environment.

We hope that we have made you think about self-concept as an important issue for children and the people who teach and care for them. What can you do that is more important for anybody than to help them feel good about themselves?

We cannot emphasise too much how important you are to the children in your care. Look at it this way...

Maybe you work in an adult/child ratio of 1 to 5, 1 to 15, 1 to 30. However big the group the child will describe you as?

In our work we meet the same stresses that you do and experience the same disappointments when children fail to respond, the pain of feeling helpless when children seem bent on self-destruction. There is no easy answer but we hope that in this booklet we have offered you a positive approach which will help you to feel that:

You Are Powerful

You Can Help the Children in Your Care

References And Suggested Reading

AINSCOW,M. & TWEDDLE,D. (1979) *Preventing Classroom Failure.* Wylie

BALLARD. J (1982) *The Circle Book*, Irvington New York

BEVAN,K. & SHORTALL,K. (1986) *Educational Review* Vol.38, No.3

BISHOP,D.V.M. (1983) *Test for Reception of Grammar.* University of Manchester

BLISS, T. & TETLEY, J. (1993) *Circle Time*, Lucky Duck Publishing Ltd

BLISS, T., ROBINSON, G. & MAINES, B. (1995) *Developing Circle Time*, Lucky Duck Publishing Ltd

BURLAND,J.R., MENDHAM,R.P. & BROWN,T.W. (1977) *Steps to Self Sufficiency*. Chelfham Mill School, Barnstaple, Devon.

BURNS,R.B. (1979) *The Self-concept, Theory, Measurement, Development and Behaviour.* Longman

BURNS,R.B. (1982) *Self-Concept Development and Education*. Holt

CANFIELD,J. & WELLS,H. (1976) *100 Ways to Improve Self-Concept in the Classroom*. Prentice-Hall

CARLSON, N. R. (1994) *Physiology of Behaviour*. Allyn and Bacon. Boston.

CLARK,A.C. & WALBERG,H.J. (1968) The influence of massive rewards on reading achievement in potential urban school drop-outs. *American Educational Research* Journal Vol.5 No.3

ELKINS,D.P. (ed) 1976 Glad to be Me Prentice Hall

GIBBY,R.G. Sr. & GIBBY,R.G. Jr. (1976) The effects of stress resulting from academic Failure. J. *Clinical Psychology*, 23: 35-37.

GOLEMAN, D. (1995) *Emotional Intelligence*, Bantam Books

GORDON,T. (1974) *Teacher Effectiveness Training*. Peter Wyden, New York

GROSS, et al., (2000) *The Emotional Literacy Hour*, Lucky Duck Publishing Ltd

GURNEY,P.W. (1986) *Self-Esteem in the Classroom*, School Psychology International. Part 1 Vol 7, No 4 1986 Part 2 Vol 8, No 1 1987

HARGREAVES,D.H. HESTER,S.K. & MELLOR,F.J. (1975) *Deviance in Classrooms*. Routledge, Kegan and Paul

HARTLEY,R.L. (1986) "Imagine you're clever." *Journal of Child Psychology* and Psychiatry.

THE JUNIOR SCHOOL PROJECT, 1980-85 ILEA Research and Statistics Branch. London.

LAWRENCE,D. (1973) *Improved Reading through Counselling*. Ward Lock

LAWRENCE,D. (1988) *Enhancing Self-esteem in the Classroom*. Paul Chapman.

MAINES,B.J. & ROBINSON,G.S. (1988) *B/G-STEEM, a self-esteem and locus of control scale for school children aged 6-12yrs* Lucky Duck Publishing Ltd. Bristol

MEAD,G.H., (1934) *Mind, Self and Society*, Chicago Press.

MECCA,A.M., SMELSER,N.J. & VASCONCELLOS,J. (1989) *The Social Importance of Self-esteem*. University of California Press.

NASH,R. (1976) *Teacher Expectations and Pupil Learning*. Routledge Kegan and Paul.

NATIONAL CURRICULUM COUNCIL (1993) Spiritual and Moral Developemnt

PALEY,J. (1980) "Asking the wrong Question." *Community Care* No 139

PALARDY,J.M.(1969) "What Teachers Believe..What Children Achieve." *Elementary School Journal* 69, 370-374, p.259

POWER,M.J. (1967) "Delinquent Schools?", *New Society*, 19/10/67

PURKEY,W.W. (1970) *Self-Concept and School Achievement*, Prentice-Hall

REDL,F. & WINEMAN,W. (1952) *Controls from Within*. Free Press

REYNOLDS,D., JONES,D. & St LEGER,S. (1976). *Schools do make a difference*, New Society, 27/7/1976.

ROBINSON,G.S. & MAINES,B.J. (198)8 *They Can Because........ A Workshop in Print*, A.W.M.C., SEBDA Head Office, Cumbria, CA10 7YF

ROSENTHAL,R. & JACOBSON,L. (1968) *Pygmalion in the Classroom*. Holt, Rinehart & Winston.

RUTTER,M., MAUGHAN,B., MORTIMORE,P.& OUSTON,J. (1979). *Fifteen Thousand Hours: Secondary Schools and their Effects on Children*. London Open Books.

SHAW,G.B. (1912) *Pygmalion*.

WHELDALL,K. & MERRETT,F. (1988) "More sticks than carrots" *Teachers Weekly*, 9th May